I first met Zion in the Spring of 2006. We spent a month together starting colts under saddle, eating together, and discussing our faith in the Lord in every spare moment and late into the night when opportunity allowed.

Zion was hungry to soak in every word of God she could find then, and as the years went by, her pursuit only grew stronger. We have shared many long messages, prayers, and prophecies. We have also stood back to back under enemy fire.

There has never been a time that I have written to Zion that she did not respond with a powerful outpouring from God's own heart with glory given to God and intolerance of enemy deception. There is a river of God's goodness that pours forth through a well spring inside of her, honestly, like I have not found anywhere else.

Having endured such anguish in her lifetime, Zion continues to offer up a pure and generous kindness that I would only know how to describe as absolute love of Christ. I understand that Zion does not see this in herself, or at least she did not for many years–yet from the first day I met her, I did, and I have never seen anything less.

She is a walking miracle and by far, one of the most inspiring, dedicated, persevering daughters of the Most High King.

Zion can be no other way. Seldom am I found to be speechless, but as I consider words enough to honor the love of Christ, I've witnessed through her over the past years, my words fall away pale next to the light that shines through the vessel that she is.

I praise God for her friendship, I am honored because of her prayers over my life, and I am deeply impressed by her persistent holding to God's holy words of truth.

Her words will draw multitudes because they will be found true to God. Amen.

A 30-DAY DEVOTIONAL TO IGNITE PASSION FOR GOD

BOOK ONE

HEART ON FIRE

ZION LUCIER

LIFEWISE BOOKS

HEART ON FIRE
BOOK ONE
A 30-DAY DEVOTIONAL TO IGNITE PASSION FOR GOD
BY ZION LUCIER

Copyright © 2020 Zion Lucier. All rights reserved. Except for brief quotations for review purposes, no part of this book may be reproduced in any form without prior written permission from the author.

All scripture comes from Biblegateway.com.

Scriptures marked AMPC are taken from the Amplified Bible Classic Copyright © 1954, 1958, 1962, 1964, 1965, 1987 by The Lockman Foundation. Used by permission.

Scriptures marked CJB are taken from the COMPLETE JEWISH BIBLE (CJB): Scripture taken from the COMPLETE JEWISH BIBLE, copyright© 1998 by David H. Stern. Published by Jewish New Testament Publications, Inc. www.messianicjewish.net/ jntp. Distributed by Messianic Jewish Resources Int'l. www.messianicjewish.net. All rights reserved. Used by permission.

Scriptures marked NIV are taken from the NEW INTERNATIONAL VERSION (NIV): Scripture taken from THE HOLY BIBLE, NEW INTERNATIONAL VERSION ®. Copyright© 1973, 1978, 1984, 2011 by Biblica, Inc.™. Used by permission of Zondervan.

Scriptures marked NKJV are taken from the NEW KING JAMES VERSION (NKJV): Scripture taken from the NEW KING JAMES VERSION®. Copyright© 1982 by Thomas Nelson, Inc. Used by permission. All rights reserved.

Scriptures marked NLT are taken from the New Living Translation (NLT) Holy Bible, New Living Translation, copyright © 1996, 2004, 2015 by Tyndale House Foundation. Used by permission of Tyndale House Publishers, Inc., Carol Stream, Illinois 60188. All rights reserved.

Scriptures marked NLV are taken from the New Life Version (NLV) © 1969, 2003 by Barbour Publishing, Inc. Used by permission. All rights reserved.

Scriptures marked TPT are taken from The Passion Translation (TPT) The Passion Translation®. Copyright © 2017 by BroadStreet Publishing® Group, LLC. Used by permission. All rights reserved. thePassionTranslation.com

Published by:

LIFEWISE BOOKS
PO BOX 1072
Pinehurst, TX 77362
LifeWiseBooks.com

To contact the author: zionlucier.com

ISBN (Print): 978-1-952247-26-2
ISBN (Ebook): 978-1-952247-27-9

DEDICATION

To God who was with me every step of the way, Your beautiful presence surrounded me as I dug into Your Word and developed this book. You encouraged me, gave me revelation, taught me through experience and made this book happen. You are forever, and always, everything to me.

Deb,

You are a funny, witty, clever, courageous friend and I've enjoyed you so much. Thank you for being you, keep shining!! Can't wait to ride together again.

Love,
[signature]

WITH THANKS TO:

My husband, Jayden Lucier, for his constant support, encouragement and listening ear.

Sonja, for always believing in me, for the years of outpouring prayer and words of life spoken over me.

Grant, Sherry and Pauline for their encouragement in my writing.

My cousin, Heather, for her help and love.

CONTENTS

Prologue | Let Your Light Shine	1
Day 1 | Righteousness in Christ	5
Day 2 | Who Am I?	11
Day 3 | One in Christ	17
Day 4 | Holiness and Righteousness	21
Day 5 | Realness with God	25
Day 6 | Intimacy with God	31
Day 7 | Abiding	37
Day 8 | Transformation	41
Day 9 | Thanksgiving	47
Day 10 | Obstacle Course	51
Day 11 | Tenderness of God	55
Day 12 | Upward Paths	59
Day 13 | All We Need is in Us	65
Day 14 | God's Pleasure	69
Day 15 | Thoughts	75
Day 16 | Smooth Talking Seductress	79
Day 17 | Important Choice	85

Day 18	Ending the Curse with the Spirit of Holiness	91
Day 19	The Coming King	95
Day 20	Vision	99
Day 21	Anchored to the Rock	103
Day 22	Trusting When We Do not Understand	107
Day 23	Forgiven and Free	113
Day 24	Over the Mountain	119
Day 25	Pressure Reveals	123
Day 26	Importance of Faithfulness In Trials	129
Day 27	Purifying Fire	135
Day 28	Soul's Victory	141
Day 29	The Power of God's Word	147
Day 30	Tenacity	153
About the Author		159
Works Cited		163

PROLOGUE
LET YOUR LIGHT SHINE

I want to share how this devotional came to be, to encourage you to pursue your gifts and callings as God enables.

A year ago, I was excited to put my writings together and make a devotional. I did, only to find the process of book publishing to be more than I could afford. I told God if He made a way, or provided the money, I would reconsider the idea. The book sat for a year and I lost every desire to get it published. Then a job came my way that provided the funds and shortly after that, the desire to publish resurfaced.

I struggled for a couple weeks wondering if I should proceed with the process. Is it God's will?

Am I wasting my money in publishing? Am I pursuing my own desires instead of God's? Is it okay to follow the desires of my heart and move forwards with the book? I went back and forth with the decision.

One morning I was spending time with God and the parable of the talents came to mind from Matthew 25:14-40. I realized I was acting like the scared person who hid his talent out of fear of his Master. God gave me the talent for writing and the desire to move forwards with it, so why not do it?

I finally understood I did not need to be afraid of God's disapproval if He did not want me to do the book. He was perfectly capable of closing the door, giving me a dream not to proceed, or taking away the desire in order to show me another path.

God is the greatest encourager we can ever encounter. He backs our every effort, every step of the way. If it is not His timing, He will make it clear. Fear of God should never be what is holding us back. I now know I do not have to be afraid of running ahead of God and missing

His timing. I do not need to worry about not pleasing Him or doing wrong. He is not a fearful Master. He is good, loving and kind and He has a thousand ways to hold us back if He needs to.

As my husband told me in the past, "God can work through our emotions. And if we have the desire to do something, that could be God showing us through our emotions."

It would be nice to hear an audible voice or have a vivid dream to encourage us to move forward, but not everyone has that. It could be as simple as God accomplishing His will through us by giving us the desire to proceed. Let us not hold back and cower in fear but move upwards and onwards with God. It is God who gives us the desires and talents to do His will and advance the Kingdom.

> *Lord Yahweh, you will establish peace and prosperity for us, for all we have accomplished is the result of what you work through us. (Isaiah 26:12, TPT)*

The purpose of this devotional is to ignite your heart on fire for God, to awaken a deep desire in your heart to know Him better and inspire a relentless pursuit of Him, His Son, and Spirit. There is nothing better than being best friends with your Creator, God Himself. May your passion for God be ignited and your heart eternally burn for Him.

DAY 1
RIGHTEOUSNESS IN CHRIST

I want to begin with an especially important and foundational teaching–our righteousness in Christ. I ask that you please keep this first devotion in mind when you read the others to follow, because I do not want you to attempt to earn your way to God.

Our walk with Christ is not a walk of our own works to gain righteousness. No matter how much we pray, read the Word, follow dietary restrictions, or any other rule. They will not add one bit to our righteousness in the eyes of a holy God. (Romans

3:20) We cannot earn our forgiveness, salvation, or healing.

In fact, if we try to earn our salvation through any form of works, we are telling God His Son died in vain. If there was a way to earn our own righteousness, God would not have needed to sacrifice His Son for our sakes. (Galatians 2:21)

There is one way to God's righteousness, one way to salvation, and being made right with God. That one door is through belief in Jesus.

> *…that if you confess with your mouth the Lord Jesus and believe in your heart that God has raised Him from the dead, you will be saved. For with the heart one believes unto righteousness, and with the mouth confession is made unto salvation. (Romans 10:9-10, NKJV)*

When we have faith in Jesus as our Lord and Saviour, His righteousness is given to us.

> *For the Christ is the end of the law. And because of him, God has transferred his perfect righteousness to all who believe. (Romans 10:4, TPT)*

As soon as we believe in Jesus as our Saviour, His righteousness is freely given to us and we are no longer drowning in guilt because of our sin. Rather we are righteous and forgiven because Jesus died on the cross in our place, (He took the penalty we deserved). His blood was shed to wash us clean of sin, making us innocent and righteous in His sight.

> *Because of the blood of Christ, we are bought and made free from the punishment of sin. And because of His blood, our sins are forgiven. His loving-favor to us is so rich. (Ephesians 1:7, NLV)*

Because of what Jesus did for us, we no longer deserve the punishment of sinners. We see that sin reaps serious consequences.

But it was because of our rebellious deeds that he was pierced and because of our sins that he was crushed… (Isaiah 53:5a, TPT)

> *…Sin entered human experience, and death was the result… (Romans 5:12, TPT)*

Because Jesus has made us righteous, we now deserve the reward of the righteous. We will talk more about this tomorrow, but here are brief examples of what the righteous deserve:

> *He endured the punishment that made us completely whole, and in his wounding we found our healing. (Isaiah 53:5b, TPT)*
>
> *…but the gift of God is eternal life in Christ Jesus our Lord. (Romans 6:23b, NKJV)*

PRAYER

Jesus. we thank You for taking our sin and giving us Your beautiful righteousness. Help us to know how righteous and loved we are in You, Jesus, to the depth of our beings. I pray You heal us to the depth of our souls, heal us of wounds that we do not even know we have. Let Your Word penetrate each of us so deeply, bringing freedom, healing and victory in every area and aspect of our lives.

Jesus, as we read Your Word, help us hear Your voice speaking directly to our hearts, bringing light, revelation, and freedom because of Your truth. Thank You for wrapping us in Your peace and washing away every uncertainty with Your beautiful Word as we read these words. You are everything. You are the purpose and point of everything. We give ourselves and dedicate all we are to You.

We ask it in Your name, Jesus, Amen.

DAY 2

WHO AM I?

Everywhere we look in this world, there are leaders with varying opinions and ideas of what truth is. Everywhere we look there seems to be different morals and ideas of what is right and what is wrong. Who do we believe? What is truth? Can I really choose if I am a man or woman? Who am I? What am I? How do I know? Where do I turn?

I love how John says:

> *I have written you these things so that you may know...* (1 John 5:13a, CJB)

The Word of God is given to us so we may know and understand. Apart from the Word, we are anchorless, adrift in a world of confusion and various opinions. But as we read the Word, we find out who we really are. The Word is given to us *so that we may know!* We will know right from wrong, truth from lies, and who we really are.

Here are some truths we find out about ourselves as we read the Word of Truth:

- We are overcomers and have the victory in Christ. (1 John 5:4-5; 1 Corinthians 15:57)
- We are a new creation and dearly loved. (2 Corinthians 5:17; Romans 8:38-39)
- Jesus came to give us life in abundance. (John 10:10)
- Jesus came and gave us freedom from sin and death. (Romans 8:1-2)

Another truth I want to highlight again, from the Word of God, is that we are righteous through faith in Christ. It does not matter if we have a bad day and do not feel righteous. Righteousness was given to us who believe in Christ as a free gift. Here is a verse highlighting the truth of our righteousness in Jesus Christ:

> *But now, independently of the law, the righteousness of God is tangible and brought to light through Jesus, the Anointed One. This is the righteousness that the Scriptures prophesied would come. It is God's righteousness made visible through the faithfulness of Jesus Christ. And now all who believe in Him receive that gift. (Romans 3:21-22a, TPT)*

With these truths in mind, I encourage you to dig into the Word to find out the truth of what God says about you. I so enjoyed reading Psalms and Proverbs and taking note of every promise that is given for the righteous. I learned early on that those who believe in Christ *are* righteous (as stated above), and therefore, all the promises for the righteous were and are for me!

Here are some promises for you, who believe in Jesus as your Saviour, taken from Psalms and Proverbs, to get you started:

> *The path of the righteous is like the morning sun, shining ever brighter till the full light of day. (Proverbs 4:18, NIV)*

The fear of the wicked will come upon him, and the desire of the righteous will be granted. (Proverbs 10:24, NKJV)

The righteous is delivered from trouble, and it comes to the wicked instead. (Proverbs 11:8, NKJV)

In the house of the righteous there is much treasure, but in the revenue of the wicked is trouble. (Proverbs 15:6, NKJV)

The Lord is far from the wicked, But He hears the prayer of the righteous. (Proverbs 15:29, NKJV)

The name of the Lord is a strong tower; The righteous run to it and are safe. (Proverbs 18:10, NKJV)

For You, O Lord, will bless the righteous; With favor You will surround him as with a shield. (Psalm 5:12, NKJV)

The righteous cry out, and the Lord hears, and delivers them out of all their troubles… Many are the afflictions of the righteous, But the Lord delivers him out of them all. (Psalm 34:17,19, NKJV)

I was young and now I am old, yet I have never seen the righteous forsaken or their children begging bread. (Psalm 37:25, NIV)

Light is sown for the righteous, And gladness for the upright in heart. (Psalm 97:11, NKJV)

PRAYER

Jesus, I ask You to lead and guide Your people into truth as they read Your Word. Speak to their hearts as they read and come to know fully who You made them to be. Reveal Yourself to them through Your Word. Reveal their destiny and purpose. Cause them to be anchored firmly in Your Word of truth so that they can never be shaken in who You made them to be.

Please uproot every lie they have ever believed about themselves and replace it with Your glorious truth. We love You, Jesus. You are merciful, gracious, and true. Teach us to delight ourselves in You and lead us into a deeper relationship with You. We thank You for the deep, mighty, and faithful work You are doing in us.

Amen.

DAY 3

ONE IN CHRIST

Yet, Christ paid the full price to set us free from the curse of the law. He absorbed it completely as he became a curse in our place. For it is written: "Everyone who is hung upon a tree is doubly cursed." Jesus, our Messiah, was cursed in our place and in so doing, dissolved the curse from our lives, so that all the blessings of Abraham can be poured out upon even non-Jewish believers. And now God gives us the promise of the wonderful Holy Spirit who lives within us when we believe in him. (Galatians 3:13-14, TPT)

I love these verses. It is so clear that Jesus took the curse from our lives, He came to give us life more abundantly. (John 10:10) He delights in our prosperity. (Psalm 35:27) No longer must we reap the consequences of sin which brought the curse upon us. Rather we reap all the blessings.

The above passage in Galatians 3 always reminds me of a teaching I heard years ago by Patricia King. In the teaching, she explained that all the blessings found in Deuteronomy 28 were meant for all believers in Christ. Because we are wrapped in His righteousness, forgiven of sin, the curses found in that chapter no longer pertain to us. But all the blessings are ours. I enjoyed reading that chapter repeatedly, knowing all those promises of blessing are mine!

I also like the Galatians 3 passage which states that *all the blessings of Abraham are upon us.* Over ten years ago, I did a search in the Bible trying to find proof that the blessings of Abraham were upon me. Since I am not Jewish, I wanted to know if I still qualified for the blessings of Abraham. As if Galatians 3:14 was not enough, I found abundant proof here as well:

> *Therefore know that only those who are of faith are sons of Abraham. There is neither Jew nor Greek, there is neither slave nor free, there is neither male nor female; for you are all one in Christ Jesus. And if you are Christ's, then you are Abraham's seed, and heirs according to the promise. (Galatians 3:7, 28-29, NKJV)*

I learned that because I had faith in Christ, I was indeed Abraham's seed and all the blessings, promises and prophecies originally meant only for the Jews, were for all who believe in Christ—Jew and Gentile alike! There is a lot of revelation to be had when you do a study of every single promise, prophecy, and blessing that God promised to Abraham and his seed. There is a promised land to be had, and many prophecies to be fulfilled. They are not only meant for the Jews, but for all who have faith in Christ!

PRAYER

Lord, thank You that You have made every believer in You one—Jew and Gentile, male and female alike. Thank You that all the promises for Abraham and his descendants belong to all who have faith in You. Thank You that You cause us to possess every single one of the gates of our enemies. (Genesis 22:17)

Please break open the promises, prophecies and blessings You've given to the seed of Abraham and help us to know they are ours. Help us to understand them and believe them to the depth of our beings. Thank You for pouring Yourself out to us so freely, Jesus, and taking the curse from us. You have given us so much, help us to comprehend the depth of all You have done for us.

I ask in Your name Jesus. Amen.

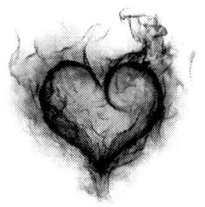

DAY 4

HOLINESS AND RIGHTEOUSNESS

If we are righteous in Christ, and cannot add or take away from righteousness because it is a gift of grace, not earned by works, then what is the point of doing anything? Do we add to our righteousness by reading the Word or praying? Are we more righteous when we do things for other people? The answer to those questions is a resounding no!

That does not mean we do not do those things. Yes, there is righteousness, but there is also holiness. Righteousness is a free gift that we cannot add to. Holiness is a process.

For by one sacrifice he has made perfect forever those who are being made holy. (Hebrews 10:14, NIV)

He gave up his life for her to make her holy and clean, washed by the cleansing of God's word. He did this to present her to himself as a glorious church without a spot or wrinkle or any other blemish. Instead, she will be holy and without fault. (Ephesians 5:25b-27, NLT)

Your Word is truth! So make them holy by the truth. (John 17:17, TPT)

Being made holy is a process. It does not happen in the blink of an eye. Why is this important? Christ Jesus is returning for a pure Bride–holy, without spot or blemish. He already has a righteous Bride, covered in His righteousness, but He is returning for a Bride made completely holy, and this holiness is a process.

One of the ways to be made holy is through the Word of God. (Ephesians 5:26) The truth of the Word will change us into a different person, as we decree it, meditate on it, and transform our minds with it.

Many of these devotions show the process of being made holy. So please do not mistake all I talk about as trying to earn righteousness. We already are righteous through our faith in Jesus, and all the promises for the righteous are already ours. Rather, what I talk about is the process of being made holy–pure and ready for the return of our King.

> *So builders beware! Let every builder do his work carefully, according to God's standards. For no one is empowered to lay an alternative foundation other than the good foundation that exists, which is Jesus Christ! The quality of materials used by anyone building on this foundation will soon be made apparent, whether it has been built with gold, silver, and costly stones, or wood, hay, and straw.*
>
> *Their work will soon become evident, for the Day will make it clear, because it will be revealed by blazing fire! And the fire will test and prove the workmanship of each builder. If his work stands the test of fire, he will be rewarded. If his work is consumed by the fire, he will suffer great loss. Yet he himself will barely escape destruction, like one being rescued out of a burning house. (1 Corinthians 3:10b-15, TPT)*

These verses accurately describe the righteousness we already have and the process of holiness. If we truly believe in Jesus as our righteousness, but waste our time or have wrong motives for works we do and neglect the journey of holiness, we will still be saved but only as ones who barely escape destruction. If we have our lives built upon the firm foundation of righteousness in Christ, and then progress in holiness through different ways, then our works of holiness will stand through fire and our reward will be great.

PRAYER

Lord Jesus, make our foundation firm and secure upon You and You alone. Let all we do flow forth from the foundation we have built upon You. Give us Your heart's desire to progress in holiness. Be our all in all and help us to move and live and have our being out of You. Jesus, give us such intense desire to pursue You and know You intimately, for everything flows forth from the intimacy found in You.

Thank You, Jesus, Amen.

DAY 5
REALNESS WITH GOD

It is important not to hide sin in our hearts or to have secret unconfessed sin. As you read these verses from Psalm 32, you will see how secret, unconfessed sin, can destroy your life. It will affect every part of your life, your emotions, spirit and physical body. But when you confess your sins, freedom comes and His forgiveness and love surround you, giving you sweet peace and relief.

> *How blessed and relieved are those who have confessed their corruption to God! For he wipes their slates clean and removes hypocrisy from their hearts. Before I confessed my sins, I kept it all inside;*

my dishonesty devastated my inner life, causing my life to be filled with frustration, irrepressible anguish, and misery.

The pain never let up, for your hand of conviction was heavy on my heart. My strength was sapped, my inner life dried up like a spiritual drought within my soul. Then I finally admitted to you all my sins, refusing to hide them any longer. I said, "My life-giving God, I will openly acknowledge my evil actions" And you forgave me!

All at once the guilt of my sin washed away and all my pain disappeared! This is what I've learned through it all: All believers should confess their sins to God; do it every time God has uncovered you in the time of exposing. For if you do this, when sudden storms of life overwhelm, you'll be kept safe. (Psalm 32:2-6, TPT)

You may be in a place where you have confessed your sins and there is nothing more to confess. That is wonderful! But notice how the psalm points out that there is a time of exposing. If you are not sure of any sin to confess now because you are not aware of any, then do not confess any. Rather wait for the time of exposing.

The time of exposing may come in the form of a trial. Sudden pressure may develop, and when the pressure is on, the deep things come up.

> *He reveals the deep things of darkness and brings utter darkness into the light. (Job 12:22, NIV)*

There are deep things in your soul that you are not even aware of, and only the pressure of tribulation can reveal them. Pressure may come and you find yourself angry, impatient, swearing, doubting God etc. This is all sin that needs to be confessed and repented during this time of exposing.

> *But if we freely admit our sins when his light uncovers them, he will be faithful to forgive us every time. God is just to forgive us our sins because of Christ, and he will continue to cleanse us from all unrighteousness. (1 John 1:9, TPT)*

I encourage you today to open your heart before God. Tell Him every little thing you think and feel. During a fiery trial, when sin raises its ugly head, I encourage you to tell Him everything like

He is a best friend. Do not numb yourself through various avenues or vices like TV, comfort food, drinking etc., because of the pain of sin. Rather, spill your heart out to Him, even if it means you sob as you talk. Out of relationship and intimacy, tell Him everything so He can heal you and set you free.

Many times, I have been through intense pain. Yet I refused to do anything to numb that discomfort. Instead, I poured out my pain and ugliness at God's feet. I shared my entire heart with God, no matter how ugly it seemed. It was after some of these times that I experienced greater joy and freedom then I ever had before. Intimacy with God in everything is key.

PRAYER

God, please help us to know to the depth of our beings, that You are here for us as a best friend. Jesus, You died and rose for the sole purpose of restoring us back to relationship with the Father with nothing separating us. Help us to walk in this kind of relationship. Grant us abundant grace to be able to be as close to You as possible.

Give us strength not to numb the pain that comes up in the time of exposing. Whether it be pain of doubt, anger, fear, abandonment, rejection, torment or anything else. Help us to face it head on, running straight to You and pouring our pain and tears at Your feet.

Holy Spirit, reveal any sin we are committing, even that we are not aware of, and convict us of it. Thank You, Lord Jesus, that as we confess our sin to you, You are faithful to cleanse and heal, wrapping us up in You. Thank You for Your righteousness that has been freely poured out upon us.

You are a good and faithful Lover and Friend. Amen.

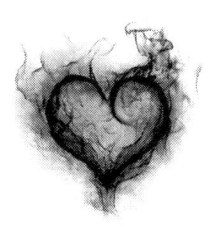

DAY 6

INTIMACY WITH GOD

One day, I felt prompted to read a bit of *The Torch and the Sword*, by Rick Joyner, and I came across these words:

> "Enoch yearned for what Adam had lost. He walked with Me, and I began to teach him like I did Adam. He discovered the source of life, walking with Me. The life became so great in him that he would have still remained on the earth if I had not brought him up to dwell with Me here. He was too full of life to die, so I had to take him up."[1]

This reminded me that intimacy with God is key–to go after the source of all life, to love Him with all that is in us, to desire Him above all else. Nothing is more important than intimacy with the Father. He gave us Himself, through Jesus, to restore our relationship to Him and have that same intimacy Adam had before sin and more as there is a whole new creation now. He is worth loving and pursuing more than anything else. This is also the greatest command:

> *Jesus replied: "Love the Lord your God with all your heart and with all your soul and with all your mind" This is the first and greatest commandment. And the second is like it: "Love your neighbor as yourself." All the Law and the Prophets hang on these two commandments. (Matthew 22:37-40, NIV)*

Here is an example of this kind of love and intimacy we are called to follow:

> *As Jesus and the disciples continued on their journey, they came to a village where a woman welcomed Jesus into her home. Her name was Martha and she had a sister named Mary. Mary sat down attentively*

before the Master, absorbing every revelation he shared.

But Martha became exasperated by finishing the numerous household chores in preparation for her guests, so she interrupted Jesus and said, "Lord, don't you think it's unfair that my sister left me to do all the work by myself? You should tell her to get up and help me."

The Lord answered her, "Martha, my beloved Martha. Why are you upset and troubled, pulled away by all these many distractions? Are they really that important? Mary has discovered the one thing most important by choosing to sit at my feet. She is undistracted, and I won't take this privilege from her." (Luke 10:39-42, TPT)

Mary gives us a beautiful example of love and dedication to Jesus. She chose to follow the most important commandment. Because of this, Jesus defended and protected her from Martha's annoyed words. If we sit at Jesus' feet, daily choosing Him over other things and cultivating intimacy with the Father and Son, He will also defend and protect us. His presence will be a shield around us (Psalm

7:10), and He will jealously protect us from every attack and lie of the enemy. (Psalm 61:3)

Mary chose the best path, the narrow path. If we want to follow Jesus on the narrow path, we must learn to sit at His feet, learning from Him and cultivating our relationship with Him. Staying close to God in relationship will protect us from many attacks of the enemy. This closeness in relationship is the path to true, fullness of life. This is the most important thing we can ever do.

> *Love the Lord your God with every passion of your heart, with all the energy of your being, and with every thought that is within you. (Matthew 22:37, TPT)*

PRAYER

Lord, help us to love and pursue You more then anything. Cause the biggest desire of our heart to be as close to You as possible. Let everything we do flow out of relationship with You. Thank You for helping and enabling us to put You first and seek after You with all that is within us.

I ask for mercy and grace to be poured upon us in abundance so that we are able to love You first and foremost. Thank You for stirring our hearts deeply with an intense yearning for You. Lord, please pour out Your love upon us in fullness of intensity.

Thank You for the good and faithful friend You are. Amen.

DAY 7

ABIDING

I know I am not the only person who has spent years decreeing the healing Word of God, but not necessarily seeing the results I expected or desired. For example, I have had a longstanding issue with my sinuses and ears for over ten years now despite constantly standing on the Word, decreeing it, and trusting God for healing.

It can be quite confusing when we do not experience the healing we desire knowing that the Word says that by His wounds we *have* been healed. (1 Peter 2:24) So why hasn't it manifested in our lives?

Yet, it is not all about our efforts. We cannot put God in a box and guarantee a certain formula will move His hand on our behalf. Everything must be done out of relationship with God and His Son. Relationship and intimacy are the most important aspects of everything we do in our Christian walk. I am where I am today, only, and all because of my relationship with God, not because of all the things I have done.

The things we do must be a biproduct of relationship with God and not a replacement for relationship. The following verses will show the importance of union (relationship) with God (Jesus, and the Holy Spirit), and how They aid in our healing and in our walk to complete freedom.

> *…for as you keep walking forward on God's paths all your stumbling ways will be divinely healed! (Hebrews 12:13, TPT)*

> *I am the sprouting vine and you're my branches. As you live in union with me as your source, fruitfulness will stream from within you—but when you live separated from me you are powerless. (John 15:5, TPT)*

Gaze upon him, join your life with his, and joy will come. (Psalm 34:5a, TPT)

You will notice in both of these verses, it's a continuous moving forward with God and abiding in Jesus that brings healing and produces fruitfulness.

Here is another example:

By his stripes (scourging) we are healed. (Isaiah 53:5b, NKJV)

Brian Simmons, author of The Passion Translation, explains:

"The Hebrew word for stripes (scourging) is chaburah and means 'blueness of the wounds.' But chaburah is taken from the root word, 'chabar' which means 'to join together, to unite, to have fellowship, to become a couple…The translation of Isaiah 53:5 could actually be – '*The fellowship of being one with him is our healing!*'" [1]

I love this! It is in our continual fellowship with Jesus that we find our full healing. I encourage you to stay remarkably close to God, Jesus and the Holy Spirit. As you abide and walk with them daily, you will grow in every area of your life, and every stumbling block will be healed.

The Kingdom of God will get bigger and bigger in you until you can no longer contain it. Then it will come bursting out of you. In the process of all this happening, you will be healed in every area and aspect of your life. Jesus will lead you onwards and upwards into the fullness of His salvation.

PRAYER

Reader, I decree a strong and tenacious faith in you to arise, causing you to cling tightly to Jesus daily. I pray you refuse to quit or let go no matter what.

Lord, I ask for mercy and grace on Your people. Help them cling to You tightly and remain in close relationship to You. It is in this deep and intimate relationship with You where the source of their full healing and salvation is found.

Thank you, Jesus, Amen.

DAY 8

TRANSFORMATION

What do you dream about every night and day? Do you dream you can fly? Do you dream things that seem ridiculous to normal people? Do you dream about glorious freedom and the amazing things you can do? Yet what does your present life look like? Do you appear to be in a cage? Is everything in your life contrary to the crazy amazing things that you dream?

I wonder what a caterpillar dreams about. While he crawls around and sees those butterflies flying above him, does he dream of flying? I wonder if he thinks he is crazy because he dreams of flying all the time.

He must say to himself, "Here I am crawling around, yet dreaming I can fly. What is wrong with me? Why can't I just accept I am a caterpillar and will always crawl? Why do I always dream I can fly?"

Yet the caterpillar cannot accept it, he just cannot stop dreaming about flying.

Does this remind you of anyone? Do you tell yourself to just accept your ordinary life? To accept that you will always be trapped in a cage, unable to spread your wings and do the things you long to do? Well I have news for you, the very thing that caterpillar thought was impossible to become... he became! Truly the impossible became possible.

Are you in a dark place? Do tears drench your face day and night? Do you feel so very alone? Are you hurting? It is okay, my friend. You are in your cocoon and an amazing transformation is taking place. Do you think the caterpillar was overjoyed to be in his cocoon?

He could be thinking, "What is happening to me? I used to dream of flying but all I could do was crawl. Now I am in a dark place where I cannot even crawl!"

The dark place you may be in could possibly just be a cocoon. The cocoon is worse than just being a caterpillar crawling around. In the cocoon, he cannot even crawl. Perhaps things feel worse for you then ever. Is there more pressure then ever before? Be encouraged, you may be in your cocoon, about to break forth. God is transforming you! (Romans 8:18)

Do you think transformation and growth is fun? I don't think the baby enjoys coming out of the warm womb into a cold world; yet that is growth. That is maturity. You are passing from one place into the next and going from glory to glory.

Do not condemn yourself if you think you should be farther or doing better than what it appears you are. Ephesians 1:18 tells us that only knowing (perceiving) our calling is enough. It does not say you have to make yourself do it, it just says you need to know it. It is also okay if you do not know it yet. Stay close to God and He will reveal it to you in His time. Just be like the caterpillar who dreamed of flying.

What a crazy impossible dream! A caterpillar flying? If he told his friends he was going to fly, they would have never stopped laughing at him.

They would have said, "You fly? Yeah, right, all you can do is crawl. Give it up, it will never happen!"

The caterpillar had no idea how he would possibly fly, but it dreamed anyway.

The Bible says that we are created in Christ Jesus to do good works. (Ephesians 2:10) As you remain abiding in Christ, God is creating you. 2 Corinthians 5:21 says we are made the righteousness of God in Him. You are made and formed and created by God as you remain in Christ.

> *Know that the* Lord *is God. It is he who made us, and we are his; we are his people, the sheep of his pasture. (Psalm 100:3a, NIV)*

Do you understand? It is God who makes us. Just remain in Christ Jesus and let God do His good work in you. Trust God and do not run from what He is doing, just keep going and the world will be in awe of what God does in you. Christ Jesus is our cocoon and we are being transformed into His glory as we remain in Him.

PRAYER

God, I ask for grace and mercy on Your people to break forth and break out of their cocoon. I decree a breaking out and breaking forth of Your fullness in them. It is written You are Your people's portion. Your fullness is Your people's inheritance, released through Jesus Christ's death and resurrection.

Jesus, I ask You to arise and shine out of Your people now, in fullness of glory. Show the world what You do for those who love You and make a huge distinction between Your faithful lovers and those who do not believe. Cause Your lovers to shine so brilliantly that wherever they go they turn people's dark nights into glorious mornings. Wherever they go, flowers bloom, salvations spring forth and healings happen. I ask for courage on Your beloved ones to keep going and strength to break forth into utter freedom of the resurrected Lord.

In Jesus' name. Amen.

DAY 9

THANKSGIVING

Don't be pulled in different directions or worried about a thing. Be saturated in prayer throughout each day, offering your faith-filled requests before God with overflowing gratitude. Tell him every detail of your life, then God's wonderful peace that transcends human understanding, will make the answers known to you through Jesus Christ. (Philippians 4:6-7, TPT)

I love these verses and have often lived by them; I tell God every detail of my life. I very much enjoy talking to Him and spending time with

Him, and that's reason enough to do it. But also, the verse says if we tell Him every detail of our lives, He will give us His peace and make His answers known in every situation, through Jesus.

I read something the other day, and it made me realize I missed an ingredient. The above verses tell us to share everything with Him with overflowing gratitude (other translations say thanksgiving). I realized I was missing the continual thanksgiving part in my life and determined to add it in immediately.

In obedience to the Word, I began telling Him everything and added in a lot of praise and thanksgiving. I started thanking Him for what He was doing and had done. I thanked Him for answering, caring and hearing. I thanked Him for His love and goodness. I surrounded everything I told Him about with thanksgiving.

Immediately when I started doing this, I felt His presence much stronger. There was so much peace in His presence, I felt a soaring in my heart and an assurance He heard what I told Him. It seemed to change the atmosphere around me.

If you are like me and tell Him every detail of your life, expecting to feel His peace and see His answers (as the verse says you will), do not forget the thanksgiving part. Remember, God's people of old did not enter the promised land because of their grumbling and complaining. Let us not be like them.

I wanted to point out another verse that shows the power of praise and thanksgiving.

> *You have built a stronghold by the songs of babies. Strength rises up with the chorus of singing children. This kind of praise has the power to shut Satan's mouth. Childlike worship will silence the madness of those who oppose you. (Psalm 8:2, TPT)*

Our genuine childlike worship and thanksgiving have the power to bring an end to the enemy's work in our lives. Let us not take these valuable weapons for granted.

PRAYER

Lord, I ask You to give us strength and reminders to thank You for everything we can think of. I ask You to fill our hearts with joy as we thank and praise You. Father, you use our praise as a weapon to destroy the enemy in our lives. Thank You, Jesus, for Your goodness, mercy, grace, presence, protection, glory and love.

Amen

DAY 10

OBSTACLE COURSE

I was reading these words in Hebrews when God spoke to me:

As for us, we have all of these great witnesses who encircle us like clouds. So we must let go of every wound that has pierced us and the sin we so easily fall into. Then we will be able to run life's marathon race with passion and determination, for the path has been already marked out before us. (Hebrews 12:1, TPT)

The footnote with this verse around the word "race" really stood out to me. It said: "…or, 'obstacle course.' The Greek word *agona* means agony or conflict. The assumption is that this race will not be easy, but the proper path to run has been set before us."

In reading this, I realized we sometimes feel we are not in God's will when the way is not as easy as we expect. We may feel God has led us somewhere down the right path. When the going gets harder, we start to wonder if we really are in God's will.

There have been many examples in my life when I have followed God's leading, but the going did not get any easier; in fact, it even got harder for a time. For example, when I lived in Kelowna, there had been many terrible emotional times. Finally, in 2017, the path finally got smoother and a little easier for a short and sweet couple of months.

I got to a place where there were not as many triggers that brought pain to my emotions and I pressed into God's beautiful presence for many hours a day with no distraction. Then I went to a conference in Kitimat and I felt like God wanted me to move there. After much pressing into God and many confirmations that it was the right choice, I went for it.

Moving to Kitimat brought new challenges and friendships that pushed my buttons and triggered more emotional pain. I felt like I had regressed because of all the painful trials that arose. Yet, those struggles and challenges caused me to grow.

I learned that just because things are not easy does not mean it is not God. There are giants to be slain as we take the promised land Jesus died and rose for us to have. We must keep fighting forwards and pressing into God. In the struggle, we break through and become that butterfly. It is in the overcoming that we become mature sons of God who are strong and mighty to destroy any enemy in our path.

PRAYER

Lord, I ask for courage for us who are going through fiery trials. Encourage us on our journey and give us strength to prevail and cling to You through it all. Help us share every part of our heart with You in these times and enable us to draw closer to You than ever before.

Thank you, Jesus, for your intense pleasure in your faithful ones who refuse to never stop believing in you. Thank you that your grace is sufficient to keep us faithful and on your straight and narrow path. Encourage us and help us to know how immense the reward is for our love to you.

In Jesus' mighty and powerful name, I ask. Amen.

DAY 11

TENDERNESS OF GOD

Sometimes we can make premature or wrong judgements. We can be opinionated, prideful, and certain that we are right. We see this in Psalm 73 with David, yet despite everything, he was treated with such deep and tender love by God. God did not turn His back on him. Rather, He drew David even closer and counseled him, leading him forth in wisdom.

> *When I saw all of this, what turmoil filled my heart, piercing my opinions with your truth. I was so stupid. I was senseless and ignorant, acting like a brute beast before you, Lord. Yet, in spite of all this, you*

> *comfort me by your counsel; you draw me closer to you. You lead me with your secret wisdom. And following you brings me into your brightness and glory! (Psalm 73:21-24, TPT)*

This is the kind of God we have! He sees beyond our faults and loves us with all our shortcomings. He pulls us close and loves us back to life. He knows the mistakes we will make but it does not deter His love for us. Rather He draws closer to us and covers our faults with His love and grace. While we are wrapped in His love, our faults are uncovered and gently revealed. But as we abide in Him and confess our sins, His love is right there to heal, mend and point us towards truth.

> *Even His grace is given as a wonderful gift. Not so we can sin, but to help us stay on His holy path. (Romans 6:15)*

> *For the grace of God has appeared that offers salvation to all people. It teaches us to say "No" to ungodliness and worldly passions, and to live self-controlled, upright and godly lives in this present age. (Titus 2:11-12, NIV)*

I love how God is not upset by our shortcomings and mistakes. He is not deterred when we get onto the wrong path. He just keeps loving us and brings us back to His path!

> *When people turn to you, they discover how easy you are to please—so faithful and true! Joyfully you teach them the proper path, even when they go astray. (Psalm 25:8, TPT)*

PRAYER

God, give us the mercy and grace to know You as You are–such an amazing, loving Father. Even when we go astray, You joyfully teach us Your paths. You have so much love and joy in us, right here, and right now. Your love is amazing. Please saturate Your people with Your love. Heal every wound and broken thing in them.

Break down every wall we have built and overtake every part of our being with Your love. We are Yours. Thank You for doing Your good work in us and knowing exactly what we need for complete healing and freedom.

You are a wonderful, gentle, and kind Father. Amen.

DAY 12

UPWARD PATHS

I was reading the other day, and came across this verse:

He opens before me pathways to God's pleasure and leads me along in His footsteps of righteousness. (Psalm 23:3, TPT)

After the word righteousness, there was a footnote that said:

> "Or 'circular paths of righteousness.' It is a common trait for sheep on the hillsides of Israel to circle their way up higher. They eventually form a path that keeps leading them higher... Each step we

59

take following our Shepherd will lead us higher, even though it may seem we are going in circles."[1]

I love this! How often does it feel like we are going in circles and not getting anywhere? Yes, sometimes our progress is obvious, but other times it feels like you try and try and do not seem to go anywhere, or even like you are going backwards.

There is one time in particular I felt this way, and everything that could be shaken in my life was being shaken. I questioned God, my faith in Jesus, and Jesus Himself, plus many other things. During that time, I read a song by Misty Edwards called *Tightrope* and was inspired to write this:

> *I thought I knew something, only to learn I know nothing.*
>
> *I thought I had a foundation built upon the Rock, but find out it's only on Sand.*
>
> *I thought I'd been shaken to my foundation before, but find out I really haven't.*
>
> *Because a tremor isn't an earthquake.*
>
> *I learned I must go backward in order to go forward.*

I've come too far to turn around; but there's still so far to go.

I have so many questions but no answers.

I can't even ask a question because there's so much swirling confusion that I no longer know what I do and don't know.

Which way's up and which way is down?

What is right and what is wrong?

I don't know anymore.

I thought I was found, only to find I'm still lost.

I'm walking a tightrope feeling like I'll fall, but there's an unseen hand ready to catch me if I slip.

I must be in His hand.

Clinging to the words of a book I always believed, but the more I read, the more questions I have.

Nothing makes sense.

Yet despite the many shakings I have been through, I know if I am going after God, believing in Jesus, thinking about Him, wanting to live for Him, fighting to know Him and share my heart with Him, reading His Word etc. Then yes, I may be circling, but I am circling upwards. It is not pointless or endless circles I'm going in; I'm going higher and higher into His glory and into His heart. I have come further than I think. Same with you.

> *But the lovers of God walk on the highway of light, and their way shines brighter and brighter until they bring forth the perfect day. (Proverbs 4:18, TPT)*

PRAYER

Jesus, thank You for leading us onwards and upwards into Your glory. I ask for mercy and grace to keep us on Your upward path. You are the hope of glory in us and I ask You to lead us onwards until You manifest the fullness of Your glory in us, causing the world to see.

Thank You for being faithful and true in every way. You are kind and merciful and so very loving. You are everything to us and we give You permission to do whatever You want and need to in our lives.

In Jesus' name. Amen.

DAY 13
ALL WE NEED IS IN US

"All the necessary ingredients are in the loaf and they are going to get stronger and stronger."

These were the words God spoke to me in April of 2014. I was about to drift off to sleep when these words came very clearly into my mind. I wrote them down, then proceeded to go to sleep.

The next day I thought about the words whispered to my mind and realized they are for every believer in Christ. Everything we could ever need is already inside of us because the resurrected Lord is inside of us. We are the temple of the living God. (2 Corinthians 13:5, 1 Corinthians 3:16)

Imagine a small seed of an oak tree. Everything is already in that seed to cause it to become a mighty tree (the roots, leaves etc). All the potential is there. You plant the seed and water it, the sun shines on it and it begins to grow. Same with us. The Kingdom of heaven is in us. It begins as a seed upon salvation, but then it begins to grow. (Luke 17:21)

That tiny seed grows as you read His Word and have faith in Jesus. Jesus gets bigger and bigger in you until you can no longer contain Him. The Kingdom grows bigger and bigger in you until you can contain it no longer. (Matthew 13:31-32) Do not worry about the growth of the seed. Do not worry if you are not yet how you want to be. All the ingredients are in you and they are growing bigger and getting stronger. Your worry and concern do not cause the growth of the oak tree, nor will it cause the growth of the Kingdom in you. Jesus is growing in you just as the Kingdom is growing in you.

He told them still another parable: "The kingdom of heaven is like yeast that a woman took and mixed into about sixty pounds of flour until it worked all through the dough." (Matthew 13:33, NIV)

Do not despise small beginnings. (Zechariah 4:10) Keep trusting God because that seed is growing in you and soon you will not be able to contain it. Soon the world will see God bursting out of you. You will arise and shine for all to see. (Isaiah 60:1-3) Just be patient with yourself as that seed matures.

PRAYER

Yeshua, I pray patience for Your people to see the amazing work You are doing in them. Encourage them with Your love and presence. Encourage them to see You are working in them and to see how far You have already brought them. Thank You for leading them and guiding them in Your paths of righteousness and glory. You are taking them ever onwards and upwards into You and not one thing will be wasted. It is all going to be worth it.

Thank You for being such an amazing, gentle and tender Saviour, loving Father and friend.

Amen.

DAY 14

GOD'S PLEASURE

Hear God saying these things to you and over you:

- I am gentle and tender and good. (Psalm 119:156)
- I see every effort you have towards me and I honour it greatly. I see you in the struggle, I see you in the trial. I see your great faith as you cling to me, refusing to let go or quit in times of greatest struggles and pain. I see you. I see you. I am the God who made the eye, and I see you. (Psalm 94:9)
- I see your love for me. I see your heart constantly crying out to me. I see and I

answer. I love you, I love your desires. You are perfect in my sight, wrapped up in the beauty of my Son. (Ephesians 1:2-3)
- I will answer your cries, I will answer your hearts plea. (Psalm 37:4)
- I am here and I answer. (Psalm 34:17)
- I am so pleased with you as you walk with me the best you know how. I am so pleased. I am a gentle and tender God and I answer, I meet you where you are at and I make a way where there is no way. (Isaiah 43:16-19)
- I am for you and not against you. (Romans 8:31)
- I will help you, I am helping you and I will give you strength. (Isaiah 41:10)
- I am here and I will see you through. Keep clinging to me, I am faithful and true and I will do it. (2 Thessalonians 3:3)
- I will not forsake you or abandon you. (Deuteronomy 31:6)
- I am here and I love you. I will reward you beyond measure as you continue running to me and clinging to me. You are everything to me. (Galatians 6:9, Ephesians 3:20)

- I am hemming you in before and behind to my plans, purposes and will. (Psalm 139:5)
- I am causing you to walk in paths of righteousness for my name's sake. (Psalm 37:31, Psalm 23:3)
- I have you with my mighty right hand and I am not letting you go. (Isaiah 41:10-13)
- You are very dear to me and I will have my way in your life. Nothing can stop me or come against me, for greater am I in you then he that is in the world. (1 John 4:4)
- I will teach you, lead you and direct you. I am training your hands for war and fingers for battle. (Psalm 18:34, Psalm 144:1, Isaiah 42:16)
- I am making you into my mighty and bold warrior, you are my weapon of war and warclub for battle. (Jeremiah 51:20)
- With you I will destroy enemy kingdoms and you will go where I say to go and do what I say to do, without a quiver of fear. (Jeremiah 1:7-10, 2 Timothy 1:7, Proverbs 28:1b)
- You cannot do it, but I can. I will erase fear from you, I will erase pain from you, just keep going. (1 Peter 2:24)

- Keep walking with me, on my path, and I will do it. (Hebrews 12:13)
- Stay faithful to me and never let go (Luke 12:8-9) and I will take you over the mountain until you conquer every enemy, just as my Son did. (Romans 8:37, Genesis 22:17) Keep on, faithful one. I love you always!

PRAYER

Lord, help me to know how much You love me. Help me to love myself that way. I ask for the mercy and grace to know how much You love me and to see myself as You see me. Help me to be patient with myself on this journey. With love comes patience, and love is patience, so I know You are increasing my patience because You are increasing my love.

Every second I spend with You increases Your mighty work in me. I am a mighty warrior after Your heart and for Your heart. Thank You for making me faithful and true and causing me to look just like You,

Jesus. Thank You for faithfully pulling me through even when I cannot keep going. You are doing an amazing work in me and I am forever grateful.

Help me to know, to the depth of my being, Your goodness, love and grace and help me manifest it and all You are to a lost and hurting world. I want to arise so close to You and set the creation free. I want to have much fruit, for the glory of Your great name.

Thank You, my King, for getting me there, in Jesus' name. Amen.

DAY 15

THOUGHTS

But to the rest of you in Thyatira who don't adhere to the teachings of Jezebel and have not been initiated into deep satanic secrets (Footnote: or have not known the deep things of Satan) I say to you… (Revelation 2:24, TPT)

Christians can sometimes get fascinated while studying conspiracy theories, other darkness and satanic secrets. Yet that is not what we are supposed to do. We are supposed to be fascinated with the things of Christ. We are supposed to be experts in all that is good and beautiful, but innocent and pure when it comes to evil.

> *I'm so happy when I think of you, because everyone knows the testimony of your deep commitment of faith. So I want you to become scholars of all that is good and beautiful, and stay pure and innocent when it comes to evil. (Romans 16:19, TPT)*

We are also supposed to keep our minds bound to all that is good.

> *Finally, brothers and sisters, whatever is true, whatever is noble, whatever is right, whatever is pure, whatever is lovely, whatever is admirable—if anything is excellent or praiseworthy—think about such things. (Philippians 4:8, NIV)*

The truth is, that whatever we think about, we become.

> *For as he thinks within himself, so is he. (Proverbs 23:7a, TPT)*

Changing our thoughts really works. I once spent three months, 3-5 hours a day, reprogramming my heart. I would sit and meditate on God and His Word, thinking only on all that is beautiful and true. I would focus on God and His presence and being with Him. I would think about nothing else. At the end of this three months, I found I had stopped worrying like I used to. In fact, at the time, I needed a place to live. My friend came and asked me if I had somewhere to stay and I said, "No."

She asked me if I was worried about what I was going to do. I searched myself and was surprised by genuinely being free of worry. I told her God would provide a place and that I was not worried. It was only a few short days later that a lady offered me her condo for a year because she was moving to Saskatchewan and needed someone to look after it while she was gone. Next time a temptation comes to follow a thread of the enemy into conspiracy theories or whatever darkness, think twice.

PRAYER

Jesus, help Your people overcome. Cause them to want You, Your beauty and purity more than anything else. Cause them to be enamoured by You, Your Son and the Holy Spirit. Let them seek after You and Your heart with all that is in them. Help Your people to be so familiar with beautiful and pure things that they recognize every work of the enemy, not by studying the enemy, but by staying close to You.

Thank You, Jesus. You are the author and finisher of your people's faith, and You complete Your work in us from the first to the last.

Amen.

DAY 16

SMOOTH TALKING SEDUCTRESS

Only wisdom can save you from the flattery of the promiscuous woman—she's such a smooth-talking seductress! She left her husband and has forgotten her wedding vows. You'll find her house on the road to hell, and all the men who go through her doors will never come back to the place they were—they will find nothing but desolation and despair.

Follow those who follow wisdom and stay on the right path. For all my godly lovers will enjoy life to the fullest and will inherit their destinies. But the treacherous ones who love darkness will not only lose all they could have had, they will lose even their own souls! (Proverbs 2:16-22, TPT)

I was reading these verses and, suddenly, I realized, this is not just talking about an adulterous woman. Yes, of course it is referring to that, but it is not limited to only this. We cannot read these verses and think we are fine because we are not that kind of woman or man. Rather, these verses could be talking to us, even if we are not adulterous or snared into the trap of adultery.

I realized the woman these verses referred to could also be sin. Sin is a smooth-talking seductress trying to draw us away from God and entice us in a trap. Sin can be whispering to us that it is okay to play for a bit, because we are saved by grace, and are righteous in Christ. It is okay to entertain a bit of darkness, a bit of swearing. It is okay to get drunk once in a while, or gossip here and there. But is it really?

Yes, it is true we are saved by grace and made righteous through faith in Christ. But that does not make it okay to *purposefully* entertain sin. Sin is so serious that Jesus tells us in Matthew 5:29

that if our eye causes us to sin, pluck it out and cast it away. In Romans, Paul tells us to surrender our bodies as instruments of righteousness and not as instruments to sin saying:

> *Don't you realize that grace frees you to choose your own master? But choose carefully, for you surrender yourself to become a servant—bound to the one you choose to obey. If you choose to love sin, it will become your master, and it will own you and reward you with death. But if you choose to love and obey God, he will lead you into perfect righteousness. (Romans 6:16, TPT)*

We use the righteousness that is given to us through Christ, to overcome every sin, *not to entertain sin*. If we entertain that smooth-talking seductress of sin, we will fall deeper and deeper into that trap and be stuck in darkness. Let us rededicate our bodies and souls as instruments of righteousness once again this day. Today is a new day to start afresh, fully and joyfully forgiven, righteous and free!

PRAYER

Jesus, we dedicate our body, mind, emotions, will, soul and spirit to You anew this day. We give every part of ourselves to You to use as Your instruments of righteousness for Your name's sake and glory. We do not want to partner with sin or entertain it any longer and we repent for all the times we have, knowing that You fully and freely forgive us. Lord, help us to feel Your joy right now, to feel Your peace, forgiveness, love and joy washing us anew. Let us experience You deeply this day, please refresh and invigorate us and cause us to love You and be committed only to You.

We choose You, just as You chose us, and we dedicate ourselves to choose You and follow You again and again, each and every day. Lord Jesus, when we fall, help us to get back up, knowing we are forgiven, knowing there is no condemnation for us who are Yours. (Romans 8:1-2, NKJV) Help us to be motivated to overcome sin because we just want to please and love

You and be the pure bride that You deserve to have. Convict us of our sin and give us the desire and power to overcome.

Thank You that You show us the way out and give us strength to take it. Thank You for Your love, for making us righteous and loving us so much. Thank You for the strength You give us and thank You for joy in the journey. Thank You for Your mercy and grace pouring over us in abundance, daily.

We ask this and thank You for it, in Your name, Jesus. Amen.

DAY 17

IMPORTANT CHOICE

Today is a new day. Today is where your book begins. You can change the course of your life right now. You are not ordinary; you do not have to do what everybody else does. You do not have to be normal and you do not have to blend in. The pen is in your hand to write this day and every other day in your life.

The Word says, in Deuteronomy 30:19, that life and death is set before us, and we can choose which one we want. We can choose which path we take. We can choose to love God or turn our back on Him. We can choose to believe in Jesus or not. We can choose to read the Word today or be too busy with life to bother. We can choose to talk to God today, and cultivate intimacy, or we can choose not to.

We can choose to change the course of our lives by choosing our thoughts carefully. We can fight thoughts of worry and darkness, or we can give into them.

> *As a man thinks in his heart, so is he. (Proverbs 23:7, TPT)*

The very things we choose to think about and meditate on, is what we will be transformed into. I love this verse as well:

> *Fill your thoughts with my words until they penetrate deep into your spirit. Then, as you unwrap my words, they will impart true life and radiant health into the very core of your being. (Proverbs 4:21-22, TPT)*

Wow! That is the power of the Word of God, as we ponder it and meditate upon it.

We also are to choose thoughts of purity and beauty as stated in Philippians 4:8. It may be hard to do this at first, and that is to be expected. We create pathways in our brains with our thoughts. The more we think about certain things, the easier and quicker our brain will turn to those thoughts, due to the pathway that has been created in the past. But over time, we can change the negative pathways in our brains to positive ones.

We may be used to worrying about finances, for example, but if we memorize a verse that counters that worry, then every time we find ourselves worrying, we can train ourselves to think on that positive verse instead. For example, we could memorize:

> *And my God shall supply all your needs according to his riches in glory by Christ Jesus. (Philippians 4:19, NKJV)*

There are so many verses of hope and life we can memorize and meditate on to counter negative thoughts and release true life into our entire beings.

Another way of choosing life is by the very words we speak.

> *For the Scriptures tell us: Whoever wants to embrace true life and find beauty in each day must stop speaking evil, hurtful words and never deceive in what they say. (1 Peter 3:10-11a, TPT)*

A man's stomach shall be satisfied from the fruit of his mouth; From the produce of his lips he shall be filled. Death and life are in the power of the tongue, and those who love it will eat its fruit. (Proverbs 18:20-21, NKJV)

Today, let us choose our thoughts and words carefully. Let us choose to draw closer in intimacy with God. We will reap a harvest according to the seeds we plant.

PRAYER

Lord, I ask You to help us choose You today. Draw us closer and closer to You and help us discipline ourselves to spend time with You every day. Even if it does not start as desire, I ask for the mercy and grace to transform our discipline into joy and delight to be with You.

As we go about our day today, please gently remind and convict us when our thoughts and words turn to anything negative. Whether it be gossip or hurtful words towards ourselves or others, please quickly remind us to hold our tongues and replace negative with positive.

Please help us to take every thought captive and choose to think on things that are pure and holy, things that are from the scriptures and give promise and hope. (2 Corinthians 10:5) Thank You for Your gentle leading, love and help.

Thank You for Your strength and encouragement to do these things. Amen.

DAY 18

ENDING THE CURSE WITH THE SPIRIT OF HOLINESS

"And I will ask the Father and he will give you another Savior, the Holy Spirit of Truth, who will be to you a friend just like me—and he will never leave you." (John 14:16, TPT)

The Passion Translation has footnotes that describe the role of the Holy Spirit in our lives. I had been desiring to know the Holy Spirit better and when I read this footnote, it helped me gain more understanding of Him and what His role is:

> "…The translator has chosen the word Savior, for it depicts the role of the Holy Spirit to protect, defend, and save us from our self and our enemies and keep us whole and healed… The Aramaic word is *paraqleta*, which is taken from two root words: (1) *praq*, "to end, finish, or to save," and (2) *lyta*, which means "the curse." What a beautiful word picture, the Holy Spirit comes to end the work of the curse (of sin) in our lives and to save us from its every effect! *Paraqleta* means "a redeemer who ends the curse."[1]

What I really took away from this was the Holy Spirit, or Spirit of Holiness, is given to us to enable us to overcome and conquer every form of sin in our lives. He is given to end the curse in our lives, and then through us, end the curse in the earth. He came to save us from every effect of the curse, making us whole and free overcomers.

Christ has redeemed us and made us righteous, but the grace He gives does not mean we should be complacent and remain stuck in sin, proclaiming by grace I am saved and I can keep sinning. No not at all. (Romans 6:1-2, 15-18) Yes, we are redeemed, righteous, and saved by grace, our faults are overlooked because we are forgiven and cloaked in the righteousness of Christ, but we do not use His grace to remain in sin. We use the grace to partner with the Spirit of Holiness and fight every stronghold of sin in our lives. With the help of the Holy Spirit, we can end the curse in our lives. Every form of sin can be conquered and overcome. We must arise and fight with the assortment of weapons given to us by God.

> *This means that God is transforming each one of you into the Holy of Holies, his dwelling place, through the power of the Holy Spirit living in you! (Ephesians 2:22, TPT)*

PRAYER

Jesus, cause us, Your beloved, to want to be holy. Let such a fire and passion burn in our hearts for purity and holiness. Cause us to want to arise and overcome every unclean thing in our lives. I ask mercy and grace to cover and enable us to overcome in every area of our lives. I pray we would have the discernment to know right from wrong and good from evil.

Lavish us in Your peace and love, Lord Jesus. Encourage us and cause us to arise and shine in the destiny You have planned for us since before the fall of Adam. Thank You, Jesus, for hearing and answering our prayers.

In Your beautiful name, Jesus. Amen.

DAY 19

THE COMING KING

The time to seek Jesus and go after the heart of the Father is now. The time to fill our lamps with oil is now. The day will come when there is no more time and people will scramble to and fro to know God, but it will be too late.

It may seem everything is going like it always has. Everyone has been talking of Jesus' return for a long time, but it has not happened. Yet His return will come like a thief in the night. The question is, are we ready? If you knew He was coming in a few months or a year, or tomorrow, would your actions be different? If we wait, saying we will seek

God another day because there is lots of time, well that is just not true. The time to seek Him is now.

There is an urgency for people to seek God now, because when His Kingdom increases on this earth and His presence becomes obvious, when His new things manifest... it is going to take a lot less faith. The reward for people will be a lot less, and there will be great sorrow in people's hearts that they did not seek Him with all their hearts, sooner. Blessed are the ones with lamps full of oil, full of faith and full of Jesus.

Let us not be like Thomas, who had to see to believe. Yes, Thomas was still accepted, yet it is more blessed to believe without seeing, and much greater the reward.

> *Jesus responded, "Thomas, now that you've seen me, you believe. But there are those who have never seen me with their eyes but have believed in me with their hearts, and they will be blessed even more!" (John 20:29, TPT)*

The time to overcome every sin, with the help of the Spirit of Holiness, is now. The time to seek Him is now. Let us not waste time. Time is a wonderful gift, but it is running out.

PRAYER

Lord, I ask You to put an urgency, joy, and desire in our hearts to seek You now with all we are. Give us strength and courage to let go of the things that are empty and help us to spend ourselves on You instead. Help us seek You, Your Kingdom, and righteousness with all our heart, strength and soul. Let us find so much joy in the journey, and addiction to Your peace and presence. An addiction that cannot be matched by any worldly thing.

You are the true healthy and glorious addiction. Help us to know and experience You with all our hearts and souls. Great is the eternal rewards for those who spend their lives completely on You. Thank You, Jesus, for Your faithful love, ever hearing our prayers and ever drawing our hearts to You.

You are faithful and true. Amen.

DAY 20

VISION

In John 13:33-38, Jesus is telling His disciples that He is going away and they cannot come with Him. He also tells Peter that Peter will deny Him. They all must have been very confused, uncertain, and hurting about all the words Jesus was saying. It did not match with what they believed was supposed to happen. Wasn't Jesus the Messiah who was going to lead them to victory? What is all this talk about betrayal and going away? What does He mean? But Jesus was not telling them this news to upset them. Rather He wanted to warn and prepare them.

We also notice that He did not leave them to wallow in the upsetting news, rather He continues the conversation giving them hope and encouragement. (John 14 and onwards) He told them not to let their hearts be troubled at the news for He was going to prepare a place for them and they would join Him where He was. He gave them a bigger vision to encourage them.

What He was saying to Peter could have sounded something like this: I know you are going to deny me, but do not worry. When it happens, think of the vision I am now giving you. Do not let your heart be troubled. I am going to prepare a place for you, and I will come again and receive you to myself. Yes, Peter you will deny me, but take heart. Just keep believing in me because I will still accept you and bring you to myself, you will get through this and you will strengthen your brothers after. (Luke 22:31-32)

He wanted the disciples to remember His words during the coming trial and, eventually, look beyond the pain to the bigger vision. This is the same example we are to follow. When we are going through trials, pain and suffering, we are to keep our eyes on the bigger vision. Jesus gave Peter vision (hope) beyond the denial, so when the denial happened Peter could (eventually) focus on the bigger picture and understand that Jesus still accepted and forgave him.

In the same way, our faith will be tested. When the testing comes, keep your eyes on Jesus. (James 1:2-4, 12) Keep your eyes on the Word and His promises. Cling to Him in faith knowing He is good and that He will see you through. A resurrection is coming.

PRAYER

Lord Jesus, I ask You to give us strength to go through the fire, and a deep realization that You are with us in the fiery furnace. Thank You for leading us through the dark night to a glorious new day. You are faithful to finish the amazing work You have begun in each of us. Give courage and strength and cause the overcoming power of the Holy Spirit to burst out of us, destroying every yoke of bondage that may be upon us.

Thank you for Your faithfulness, Jesus. I ask this in Your name. Amen.

DAY 21

ANCHORED TO THE ROCK

I had a dream that showed what it is like to be firmly established in Christ. It was a simple dream, yet impactful. I was in a house on top of a high hill overlooking the lake below. It seemed we were safe from any rising water. It would not even have crossed my mind that the water from the lake could reach us.

But through the window, I saw this huge tidal wave coming. It was a wave much larger than the hill and house I was in. I was not afraid, but I did wonder what would happen when it reached the house. When the wave came crashing over the house, I felt nothing–not even a shaking!

We know we may not be able to avoid problems in the world. Yet when our lives are hidden with God in Christ, we are utterly and completely protected. (Colossians 3:3) We do not have to fear anything. This is what it is like to be in the Kingdom that cannot be shaken. (Hebrews 12:28)

Jesus is the one firm foundation we can always count on. (Matthew 7:24-27) The most important relationship we can ever have is with Him. When everything in life is changing and moving, He stays steadfast and true. His love is unfailing and never stops, He is always there. Spending time with Him and nurturing our relationship with Him daily, is essential.

We must build every part of our lives around God. When we do, we will find no matter what we are going through, we are standing firm on the Rock, stable and secure. When the storm blows through, we will remain firm, rooted in Him, and we will come out shining.

But what if a part of our life is not built upon Him? A time may come when we must experience a shaking in our lives to expose the part we have built on sand. If our lives are built, even partly, on our own striving, effort, abilities, or desires, the time will come when that issue is exposed.

A storm may come in the form of losing a job, the death of a loved one, or the death of a hope or dream etc. But take hope. If you have Jesus, cling to Him during the storm. You may feel like a snow globe that has been shaken and everything is scattered everywhere. That is okay. It is normal! God is revealing and removing any false foundation and chaff in our lives. Keep clinging to Jesus and you will come through stronger than ever before.

> *Have the roots [of your being] firmly and deeply planted [in Him, fixed and founded in Him], being continually built up in Him, becoming increasingly more confirmed and established in the faith, just as you were taught, and abounding and overflowing in it with thanksgiving. (Colossians 2:7, AMPC)*

PRAYER

Jesus, thank You for Your lovers. Thank You for their faithful commitment to You. Draw every believer even closer to Your heart. Cause their anchor to be firm and their roots to go as deep as possible in You.

If there be any part of our lives built on sand, I ask for gentle mercy and grace to come and build that part of our lives on the Rock. Give us wisdom and discernment to know what parts are built on sand and show us how to build it upon You, our Rock. Thank You, Lord, for Your faithful love and answers. You are so good, so gentle and kind.

I ask it in Your name, Yeshua. Amen.

DAY 22

TRUSTING WHEN WE DO NOT UNDERSTAND

For if you choose self-sacrifice and lose your lives for my glory, you will continually discover true life. But if you choose to keep your lives for yourselves, you will forfeit what you try to keep. (Matthew 16:25, TPT)

Laying yourself down for the sake of God, is, partly, simply walking the path God has for you instead of making your own path. It is faith in a good God and trusting Him even when His path seems to lead away from your goals and dreams. It is knowing that God has the best in mind for you, even when His path seems to go the opposite way from yours. It is letting go of your path and embracing His.

Staying close to God will ensure that you stay on His path for you and do not wander off on another. Sometimes we can pray for something, and because it does not come in the way we perceive, we miss it. Losing ourselves for God's sake, is praying and letting His answer come in the way He wants to send it.

It can sometimes be hard not to be offended at the answer He sends. Perhaps you pray for more healing and freedom, and you have in mind exactly how it should happen. Maybe you think it should happen in an instant at a church service, but what if God brings you a new friend and the healing will happen through them, over a season? Will you miss the blessing because He did not answer you in the way you wanted?

He may ask us to move to a new location. Will we trust Him enough to take the leap of faith, believing desires will be fulfilled there? Believing healing will come as we move forwards? The story of Nahum, found in 2 Kings 5, is a good example of this. He had leprosy and almost missed his healing because of his preconceived ideas of what it should look like. But his servant convinced him to do what was asked of him by Elisha's messenger. He obeyed the instructions, and he was healed.

One morning, I was spending time with God and heard His quiet whispers. I saw the path He was leading me on. It was not the way I expected or even the way I wanted, yet I was not offended. I was surprised. His guidance seemed to lead me away from how I thought He would do it. Yet I was confident in His goodness and heart of love for me.

I knew His way to be best and I knew it would get me to my dreams and desires, while the path I had wanted to take may never get me there at all. It was a morning of embracing His path for me and letting go of self.

Surrendering your life for His sake is being willing to do it His way and not getting offended at how He chooses to answer prayers. He has great delight in you. As you choose His way and have faith that He is good, He will bring you true life as you follow Him.

> *...The blessing of heaven comes upon those who never lose their faith in me—no matter what happens! (Matthew 11:6, TPT)*

His way is best. All your dreams and desires will be fulfilled as you follow Him and His way (or He will change your heart to align with His). When a door shuts, do not always think it is the enemy. It could be God hemming you into His path and His best for you. Trust Him. Fight to trust Him. Share your heart with Him and rest in His presence knowing He has the best in mind for you. Nothing can stop His good and perfect plan for you as you follow Him in His way and His will. He will complete the good work He has started in you. (Philippians 1:6)

PRAYER

Lord, help me to trust You. Help me to recognize Your path and Your voice. Help me to follow, no matter what. I ask for strength, mercy, grace and courage, to follow You no matter where You lead. I want to please You more than anything or anyone else. Thank You for wrapping me in the righteousness of Your Son.

Thank You for making me Yours forever. I willingly lay down my path, my life, my dreams and desires for Your name's sake trusting You have better for me then I could ever have for myself. Thank You for loving me and taking me deeper into Your heart.

Thank You for hearing and answering me and pouring Your blessings out upon me.

Amen.

DAY 23
FORGIVEN AND FREE

When Jesus saw the extent of their faith, he said to the paralyzed man, "My son, your sins are now forgiven." This offended some of the religious scholars who were present, and they reasoned among themselves, "Who does he think he is to speak this way? This is blasphemy for sure! Only God himself can forgive sins!"

Jesus supernaturally perceived their thoughts and said to them, "Why are you being so skeptical? Which is easier, to say to this paralyzed man, 'Your sins are now forgiven,' or, 'Stand up and walk!'? But to convince you that the Son of Man has been given authority to forgive sins, I say to this man, 'Stand up, pick up your stretcher, and walk home.'" (Mark 2:5-11, TPT)

Through the above scriptures, I want to point out the power of forgiven sin. When Jesus forgave this man, it was equivalent to telling him to get up and walk. When the man got up and walked, it was proof that Jesus did indeed have the power to forgive sins. When our sins are forgiven everything else is taken care of. (Ephesians 1:7, Isaiah 53:4-6) Jesus, the Lamb of God, has paid our debt and taken the sins of the world. (John 1:29) For everyone who believes Jesus took their punishment, they are healed.

He himself carried our sins in his body on the cross so that we would be dead to sin and live for righteousness. Our instant healing flowed from his wounding. (1 Peter 2:24, TPT)

When our sins are forgiven, we can get up and walk. The forgiveness of sin takes care of the whole root of the problem. A good illustration of this is seen in a tree with roots. The roots of the tree are called sin, and everything going upward (leaves, fruit) is the fruit of sin. Some examples of possible fruits of sin are: deafness, blindness, paralysis, cancer, AIDS, HIV, death, depression, eating disorders, mental illness of all kinds, body pain etc. Jesus came once, for all, and ripped that tree of sin out by the root. He did this for all people, and it is accessed through belief in Him as Saviour. (Romans 10:9, Acts 16:31)

Here is another scripture illustrating this truth:

> *No one living in Zion will say, "I am sick, for all who live there will have their sin forgiven." (Isaiah 33:24, TPT)*

The people will not say they are sick, because they have been forgiven. Again, the truth is that forgiveness of sin is equivalent to being healed. But why don't we see this more often? Why is the Body of Christ, though forgiven of sin, not always showing healing in their lives? We will touch on this in days to come, but keep in mind, just because God's promises and the truth of His Word may not have manifested in our lives yet, it does not make the truth any less true!

PRAYER

Lord Jesus, thank You for forgiving my sins and making me righteous in You. Thank You that I now reap the reward of righteousness and not the reward of sin. I reap Your forgiveness, healing and blessings all because of what You did for me. It is amazing how the Father now sees me—wrapped in You, Jesus. (Ephesians 1:3)

Continually unfold this truth to me until it manifests in every area and aspect of my life. Thank You for healing me. Even though I may not see it in every area of my life yet, I know I will because Your Word is truth.

Keep me holding onto You in faith, no matter what happens in my life. Help me trust and believe You even if I do not see the healing in my life right away. Strengthen my faith in You, Your Word and Your goodness. Remove every attitude and mindset in me that is not of You. Heal every area of my life. I do not want to settle for anything less then all You died and rose for me to have.

Thank You for leading me into the absolute fullness of your salvation. (Psalm 91:16b) Amen.

DAY 24

OVER THE MOUNTAIN

Do you believe your sins are forgiven? Do you believe that Jesus died and rose to heal your body and emotions? Our faith tells us this is true, and yet it does not always seem to be manifesting in our lives. I can assure you, it is not your fault!

The Word says we enter the Kingdom through trials and tribulations. (Acts 14:22) It says if we want to be glorified with Him, we must suffer with Him. (Romans 8:17b) 1 Peter 1:6-7 tells us there will be trials so our faith will be proven, and we will come forth as gold. James 1:3-4 tells us when our faith is tested, it stirs up power in us to endure all things; and as our endurance grows, it releases perfection into every part of our being.

There is a purpose for the trials. Trials squeeze out everything in us not of God, giving us the opportunity to repent for the hidden sins that come up. Trials develop our character and develop our faith. In trials, we have a chance to cling to God in faith and show our love and loyalty for Him. This brings eternal rewards and changes in ourselves.

Do not be discouraged because the trials will not last. We must push through them and overcome each one. Trials are used for good in our lives, but we do not have to remain in them. We must go over the mountain! We confess our sin and share our heart with God in the trials. We let them develop us and purify our faith, but we do not stay there. We push onwards into glory.

In my life, I have experienced intense shakings where the difficulties and trials brought doubt towards God up in me. Doubts I did not even realize were there. In these times, I realized a part of me did not believe He was good or that He would keep His Word to me. I was often shocked at my unbelief but also grateful that God had uncovered it. As a result, I could confess to Him what was in my heart and find healing. (1 John 1:9) Also, when these doubts were revealed, I learned to strengthen myself in faith by going to the Word (verses that countered my doubts) and take His promises into my heart.

No matter where you are at, do not forget these verses:

> *If your faith remains strong, even while surrounded by life's difficulties, you will continue to experience the untold blessings of God! True happiness comes as you pass the test with faith and receive the victorious crown of life promised to every lover of God! (James 1:12, TPT)*
>
> *And tell John that the blessing of heaven comes upon those who never lose their faith in me—no matter what happens! (Matthew 11:6, TPT)*

PRAYER

Lord, I ask Your mercy and grace on Your people to endure through the trials, and to overcome. They have suffered many already. Lord, please move them through the trial and onwards into glory. I ask that You cause them to experience the victory that is on the other side of it. Please manifest it now, as quickly as possible, in their lives. Your Word says now is the day of salvation. (2 Corinthians 6:2)

Lord, You say You take those who love You on Your path of light shining brighter and brighter to the full light of day. (Proverbs 4:18) Thank You for full healing and freedom in every area and aspect of our lives as we continue onwards in intimacy with You.

Amen.

DAY 25
PRESSURE REVEALS

Peter said, "What do you mean I'm not able to follow you now? I would sacrifice my life to die for you!" (John 13:37, TPT)

I believe Peter meant what he said from the depth of his being. He really believed he would lay down his life for Jesus. Peter did not know denial was within himself until the intense pressure brought it out.

Ever been going about your day feeling good, then smacked your head, stubbed your toe, or hit your finger with a hammer and suddenly, you start swearing? You wonder where those words came from. You really did not want to say them. They only came out under pressure. This is what happened to Peter. He was sincere in his earnest words to Jesus, but when the intense trial came, fear and other things arose in Peter he did not even know he had. Despite his heartfelt words, he denied Jesus three times, later deeply regretting what he had done.

I am sure all of us would like to say we would not deny Jesus. But would we? Would we deny Him under intense duress? Pain? Torture?

> *Beloved friends, if life gets extremely difficult, with many tests, don't be bewildered as though something strange were overwhelming you. Instead, continue to rejoice, for you, in a measure, have shared in the sufferings of the Anointed One so that you can share in the revelation of his glory and celebrate with even greater gladness! (1 Peter 4:12-13, TPT)*

We are being purified by the trials, circumstances and tribulations that arise in our lives. A couple verses that illustrate this perfectly are:

> *O Lord, we have passed through your fire; like precious metal made pure, you've*

> *proved us, perfected us, and made us holy. (Psalm 66:10, TPT)*

> *I will bring my fiery hand upon you and burn you and purify you into something clean. (Isaiah 1:26, TPT)*

The fire is very necessary because God cannot use us if we are full of anger, jealousy, bitterness, pain, lies, doubt, or pride. These things block His ability to flow through our lives. If "self" is in the way, we cannot be used by Him as He desires. But God will bring us face to face with these issues in our heart through the intensity of trials so we can repent and be healed:

> *How blessed and relieved are those who have confessed their corruption to God! For he wipes their slates clean and removes hypocrisy from their hearts. Before I confessed my sins, I kept it all inside; my dishonesty devastated my inner life, causing my life to be filled with frustration, irrepressible anguish, and misery.*

> *The pain never let up, for your hand of conviction was heavy on my heart. My strength was sapped, my inner life dried up like a spiritual drought within my*

> *soul. Then I finally admitted to you all my sins, refusing to hide them any longer. I said, "My life-giving God, I will openly acknowledge my evil actions." And you forgave me! All at once the guilt of my sin washed away and all my pain disappeared! (Psalm 32:2-5, TPT)*

Just like Peter had to go through the trial and pain of denying Jesus, we also will have to go through hard things. But remember and be encouraged by Peter's comeback story! You will also come through the trials and shaking, shining brighter and being freer than ever before.

PRAYER

Lord, I thank You for trials that purify and reveal the deep things in us that are not of You so we can repent of them and find strength, healing and mercy in our time of need. I ask You to shake everything in us so our lives will be built on the Rock alone. Let everything else be removed.

Give us strength to overcome every sin so we will walk in all the promises for the overcomers and arise in the fullness of Your salvation for the world to see. Purify us into pure gold. Bring every deep thing of darkness to light in us and let Your light replace the darkness. (Job 12:22)

I ask in Jesus' name.

Amen.

DAY 26

IMPORTANCE OF FAITHFULNESS IN TRIALS

In the book of Job, we see Satan claiming the only reason Job was faithful to God, was because of God's protection around him. Therefore, God removed His hedge of protection around Job's life, allowing him to be sifted by the enemy. Job went through intense suffering, yet Satan could not get him to turn his back on God.

In the end, it was proven that Job was not only being faithful to God because of His blessings on his life, Job was a dedicated lover of God no matter what trial or persecution came his way.

As a result of Job's faithful and determined love of God (refusing to let go, clinging to Him in trials), God blessed Job more than ever before. (Job 42:12-16)

- God allowed Peter to be sifted by Satan. (Luke 22:31)
- Paul and other apostles and disciples experienced intense trials and suffering. (2 Corinthians 1:8)

Trials and tribulations are Biblical, and we will go through them. (James 1:2-4, 12) We also will have the opportunity to prove our loyalty to God just as Job and many others did. Remember, loyalty only in good times is not loyalty at all. We need to have the opportunity to prove our loyalty to God, staying faithful to Him even when it seems He has abandoned us to the intense fiery trials.

If you have not been through intense trials or under incredible pressure, how will you ever know if you will be faithful during the hard times? How will people around you be able to know your true character and depend deeply upon you if you have not been proven loyal in suffering? Take courage in your trials because you are being made into a mighty warrior!

Also, if you are going through some trials, be encouraged because this does not necessarily mean you are doing anything wrong. In fact, Job was doing everything right and he was still sifted by Satan. These trials are an opportunity to prove your love to God. And when you are proven, you will come forth with greater strength.

Remember the verses from prior devotions and do not think it strange when you go through trials. There will be a death and burial, but they will be followed by life and resurrection as you cling tightly to God in trials, refusing to quit or let go.

I read a book called *Visions From Heaven: Visitations to my Father's Chamber* by Wendy Alec. Here are some encouraging quotes from Wendy Alec's book.

> "Your clinging to Me, My beloved child, was to Us one of the greatest acts of faith in your entire earthly life." I was stunned. Anyone who would have looked at me from the outside would have come to the conclusion I had no faith. But, here in the Father's chamber, my Heavenly Father was telling me

that it was in those moments of utter desperation, clinging only to Him by the most tenuous of threads. That this was faith indeed."[1]

"I had never wept so many tears. I had never been so assailed in my mind. I had never come so close to having both my mind and my physical body and my spirit broken. I felt an incredible wave of immense overwhelming love from my Father wash over me. He spoke again. "Courage is measured here in Heaven far differently than on Earth. When My children are hit by trials and testing that push them almost to the edge of their endurance. And yet still they stand and still they endure. Still the persevere. Still they believe. That is courage indeed."[2]

"Although you have won many battles and done many exploits through GOD TV and the media and will do many more - none, none of these exploits of faith come close to My heart. My so beloved child, to the times of the greatest trial you faced through infirmity, when you walked through the valley of the shadow and abandonment - pushed almost to the very boundaries of your endurance. And yet still you did not deny Me, this is when you won the overcomers crown."[3]

PRAYER

Lord, I pray that as Your people read these words, they will find great encouragement and faith to keep pressing into You during the trials and pain. Help them to remain loyal and true to You, God, tightly clinging to You through it all. For if they do, their reward will be immeasurable. Please give them hope and courage to endure.

Amen.

DAY 27

PURIFYING FIRE

We can be encouraged when we are fighting through hard times, but continually going after God. The trials we go through are a purifying fire and they are making us mature, cleansing us of everything that is not of God. (Psalm 66:10) They cleanse us from every worry, doubt, fear, anxiety etc. This must happen because Jesus wants a pure bride fully free, healed and shining for His glory. (Ephesians 5:27)

Notice in the Bible how the fire comes before the glory:

> *Now when Solomon had made an end of praying, the fire came down from heaven, and consumed the burnt offering and the sacrifices; and the glory of the Lord filled the house. (2 Chronicles 7:1, KJV)*

This happened in the Old Covenant temple. But now His people are His temple and we can be sure the fire of trials is cleansing and purifying us, preparing us for His glory to fill the temple (us). (1 Corinthians 3:16) Here are a couple verses that show the fire comes to cleanse and purify us, making us ready for the fullness of His glory to flow in, and through us.

> *I will bring my fiery hand upon you and burn you and purify you into something clean. (Isaiah 1:25, TPT)*

> *For in a visitation of the night you inspected my heart and refined my soul in fire until nothing vile was found in me. (Psalm 17:3a, TPT)*

When we are in the night season, the fire is burning away every vile thing, until we exit the fire completely mature and pure. We also see this is the same in Jesus life, the fire (suffering of the cross) came before the glory (resurrection).

Yes, Jesus paid our penalty on the cross, and "it is finished." We now can walk in complete freedom, healing and glory. But we must go through fire to manifest the fullness of it. Jesus, Himself, told us:

"…The Son of Man must suffer many things, and be rejected by the elders and chief priests and scribes, and be killed, and be raised the third day." Then He said to them all, "If anyone desires to come after Me, let him deny himself, and take up his cross daily, and follow Me. For whoever desires to save his life will lose it, but whoever loses his life for My sake will save it." (Luke 9:22-24, NKJV)

When Jesus said, "if anyone desires to come after Me" He was referring to us following Him in resurrection life because, taking it in context, He just finished saying the Son of Man would suffer and be raised on the third day. Therefore, we can see the fire must happen before the resurrection. We must lay down our lives for Him before we can go through the glory of the resurrection.

We will experience being co-glorified with him provided that we accept his sufferings as our own. (Romans 8:17b, TPT)

The footnote for this verse says: "If we suffer jointly, we will enjoy glory jointly."[1] The principle is quite clear, just as Jesus suffered and was made perfect through suffering, we must follow Him into suffering and only then, glory. (Hebrews 2:10, 5:8-9)

PRAYER

Lord, I ask that Your people be encouraged by the fire in their lives, knowing that great glory will come after. Their reward will be You making Your home in them and them experiencing You more then ever before. Encourage them to remain standing on the Word of truth and staying faithful to You through it all. Help them to know You are bringing them through the fire, free of all stains and effects of sin, to walk in the fullness of Your resurrected glory.

Thank You that when the enemy comes into their lives to push their triggers and buttons, he will find no response. The fire will have purified them causing no offense or negative thing to arise. They will be completely purified, and Your glory will flow through them to a lost and hurting world, bringing hope and freedom wherever they go. I ask for abundant grace and mercy to flow over Your people and make this happen.

I thank You for it, Jesus. Amen

DAY 28
SOUL'S VICTORY

Don't you know that when you allow even a little lie into your heart, it can permeate your entire belief system? (Galatians 5:9, TPT)

Often when we start to follow Jesus, many lies have already been implanted into our beings from when we were a child. There can be lies of our worth and how other people see us. There can be lies causing tormenting emotions, fears and anxieties, preventing God from being able to use us as He wants. These lies have permeated our entire beings, causing freedom to seem far away.

Yet there is so much hope! Complete healing from all these issues is possible.

> *Through our faith, the mighty power of God constantly guards us until our full salvation is ready to be revealed in the last time. For you are reaping the harvest of your faith—the full salvation promised you—your souls' victory! (1 Peter 1:5,9, TPT)*

The full salvation of our souls includes our emotions, will and mind. We can have the victory in every area. We can experience a life free of guilt, tormenting emotions, fear, stress and anxiety. I once had all these things to a large degree, but through years of pressing into God and doing all the things I have shared with you in this book, I no longer have many of them.

We all can have a prospering soul, joy in abundance, and peace that is never shaken. (John 10:10b, Psalm 35:27b) We can live totally free of lies, pain and every sin and result of sin. But it will not be easy to get there. It will be a process, a fight of faith, a walk of holiness and a tenacious clinging to God. It will require dealing with all the lies by using the blood of Christ, prayer, and all the weapons God has given us to overcome. And we can overcome because Jesus died and rose for us to have complete victory and freedom in every area of our lives.

To walk in this, we cannot ignore the lies that have permeated our systems. It may seem obvious that it will be a fight to overcome, but is it? Some people believe that upon salvation, they are instantaneously healed, everything is easy, and every lie gone. Therefore, they ignore all hurt or pain in them, saying they are free and do not have to do anything. Yet their actions and insides are not saying that at all.

As children, their foundation was built on lies, and coming to Christ will not fix that in an instant. If it did, we would not be called to overcome because there would be nothing to overcome. If everything were fixed in an instant, the Word would not tell us we have to renew our minds to be transformed. (Romans 12:2)

Yes, there can be instantaneous freedom in different areas like addiction, bodies healed, or guilt gone. I know we will see more and more of that in times to come. But for the total healing of a soul, God is going to have to totally rip out the old foundation and replace it with a new one built only on His truth.

This is done through the renewing of our mind and closeness to Jesus. It is done as we rest in and trust Him, share our entire beings with Him through relationship, and through the help of others. It is done as we decree and meditate upon the Word and learn of our righteousness in Him. It is done as we go through trials, tribulations, shakings and continue to walk on the highway of holiness.

Even though it is not an easy process, I can promise it will be worth it. Complete freedom, joy, peace and love, can be walked in. We can manifest His kingdom for the world to see. We must let Him get rid of every little lie hidden in the foundation of our being until we shine with His glory, walking in the fullness of His glorious truth.

PRAYER

Jesus, help us keep trusting in You as the lies in us are ripped out and removed. Even if it comes out in anger, fear, stress or any other unhealthy emotion, help us to know we are feeling it as it is on the way out. Show us we are right in Your perfect will even if it feels bad for a time. Please replace the lie with the beauty of Your presence, truth, peace and all that You are. Make us Your home where no lying thing can ever reside.

I pray for an acceleration of time over us so that this would be a quick process. Help us to have the patience to endure it if necessary. That it be done as gentle as You are able, but as firm as needed.

Thank You for the process and all that we learn in it and that the victory is already ours. Thank You that You are with us as we walk the victory out. You have such a firm hold upon us and You will not stop Your good work in us until we stand on a firm foundation with every lie shaken out, and only Your Kingdom remains!

In Jesus' name I pray.

Amen.

DAY 29

THE POWER OF GOD'S WORD

There are ways to get through trials without getting stuck in them or getting caught in the enemy's trap. You can do this by using the power of the Word of God in your life. Let us look at some verses that show this.

> *For he died for us, sacrificing himself to make us holy and pure, cleansing us through the showering of the pure water of the Word of God. (Ephesians 5:25b-26, TPT)*

"Is not my word like fire," declares the LORD, "and like a hammer that breaks a rock in pieces?" (Jeremiah 23:29, NIV)

Take the helmet of salvation and the sword of the Spirit, which is the word of God. (Ephesians 6:17, NIV)

He sent His Word and healed them, and delivered them from their destructions. (Psalm 107:20, NKJV)

So bless the Lord, all his messengers of power, for you are his mighty heroes who listen intently to the voice of his word to do it. (Psalm 103:20, TPT)

The entrance of Your Word gives light; it gives understanding to the simple. (Psalm 119:130, NKJV)

…having been born again, not of corruptible seed but incorruptible, through the word of God which lives and abides forever. (1 Peter 1:23, NKJV)

So then faith comes by hearing, and hearing by the word of God. (Romans 10:17, NKJV)

By his own choice, he gave us birth by the word of truth so that we would be a kind of firstfruits of his creatures. (James 1:18, CSB)

And we also thank God continually because, when you received the word of God, which you heard from us, you accepted it not as a human word, but as it actually is, the word of God, which is indeed at work in you who believe. (1 Thessalonians 2:13, NIV)

Fill your thoughts with my words until they penetrate deep into your spirit. Then, as you unwrap my words, they will impart true life and radiant health into the very core of your being. (Proverbs 4:21-22, TPT)

Every Scripture has been written by the Holy Spirit, the breath of God. It will empower you by its instruction and correction, giving you the strength to take the right direction and lead you deeper into the path of godliness. Then you will be God's servant, fully mature and perfectly prepared to fulfill any assignment God gives you. (2 Timothy 3:16-17, TPT)

Then you will shine among them like stars in the sky as you hold firmly to the word of life. (Philippians 2:15b-16a, NIV)

These verses prove the incredible value and power of the Word of God, and show that the Word will heal, transform and cleanse us. It washes out every defilement and purifies us to the depth of our soul. It is like a hammer that smashes and destroys every stronghold of the enemy in our lives.

The Word is a sword the Spirit takes and fights with, for our benefit. The Word has a voice that the angels hear. As we decree it, they go forth to bring it to pass. Not only does faith come as we speak the Word of God, but we are also born again by reading and continually meditating upon it. There are infinite benefits to reading the Word. As we read it, it works powerfully in our lives to change us for the glory of God.

I encourage you to read, mediate, and decree the Word. You will never be the same! Let us take advantage of this powerful weapon. In Matthew 4, Jesus sent the enemy fleeing by speaking the truth of the Word. Jesus is a good example to follow! With the sword of the Word in our mouth, we can conquer kingdoms while snatching many souls from the enemy's clutches. We can bring light to the darkest of places and transform every aspect of our lives (and others).

> ## PRAYER
>
> Jesus, Your Word says that by Your wounds I am healed, I am victorious, and I am an overcomer. It says I am the head and not the tail. I am above and not beneath. I am complete in you—the head of every principality and power.
>
> - It is written no weapon formed against me prospers and I am a new creation. (Isaiah 54:17, 2 Corinthians 5:17)
>
> - It is written I have been buried with you in the likeness of your death and am risen with you in your resurrection life and I am more than a conqueror through you. (Romans 6:4-5; Romans 8:37)
>
> - It is written you have abolished death and brought life and immortality to

light through the gospel in my life. (2 Timothy 1:10)

- It is written I am your temple, and where you are there is only light and no darkness, therefore there is no darkness in me, only the light of your glory. (1 Corinthians 3:16, 1 John 1:5)

- It is written that He who raised Christ from the dead dwells in me and quickens my mortal body. (Romans 8:11)

I have been cleansed and set free by your blood. I am made new, I am healed, I am free. For where the Spirit of the Lord is, there is liberty! Your Word says now is the day of salvation. Now is the time for all these things to come to pass. Thank You, Jesus, for the weapon of Your Word, for setting me free and making me all for You.

In Your name, Jesus.

Amen.

DAY 30

TENACITY

Jesus rebuked the demon, and it came out of the boy, and he was healed at that moment. Then the disciples came to Jesus in private and asked, "Why couldn't we drive it out?" He replied, "Because you have so little faith. Truly I tell you, if you have faith as small as a mustard seed, you can say to this mountain, 'Move from here to there,' and it will move. Nothing will be impossible for you." (Matthew 17:18-20, NIV)

When I read this verse, it reminded me of something my husband wrote that really blessed me:

The word "littleness" or "small" could be the word "brief". Jesus was not saying, "Your faith was not big enough", He was saying "You didn't leave it in the fight long enough to win."

It does not take much faith to move mountains, it takes persistent faith! The measure, I cannot say. But what I can promise is He is faithful to see it through with you.

I pray the Lord gives you His tenacity and endurance to see your race through to the end!"

Jayden Dion Lucier

And tell John that the blessing of heaven comes upon those who never lose their faith in me—no matter what happens! (Matthew 11:6, TPT)

True faith is when we develop a faith that learns to never quit. We hang on to God, His Son and His promises with a tenacity that refuses to let go. When we do this, we are guaranteed to see the blessings of heaven rain down upon our lives. Let us have a mindset where quitting is not an option.

Remember Jesus' words that came immediately after the story of the persistent widow and the unrighteous judge in Luke 18. He asked if He would find that kind of faith on the earth when He returned. What kind of faith was He referring to? He was referring to faith like the widow. A faith that refused to quit until justice was seen. Likewise, let us have a faith that holds onto God and all that He has for us and refuse to let go until heaven's blessings rain down in fullness upon our lives, and the lives of others.

> *For the raging roar of stormy winds and crashing waves cannot erode our faith in you. (Psalm 46:3, TPT)*

Yet, in saying all this, I know "quit" can be found in us and that is okay. I thought I would never quit on God, that I did not even have it in me. But one day there was so much crushing pressure, I was ready to give up. It is okay if we reach this point because God is bringing us to the end of ourselves so we can learn to rely on His strength and ability. His grace is enough to hold us and keep us even when we are ready to quit. It is not about us and our strength or staying power. It is all about God and His grace. He is able to keep us faithful.

PRAYER

Lord Jesus, we ask for strength to go through the trials and storms of life with You and never quit. Please shake out everything in us that can be shaken, but let Your Kingdom remain. Let Your Kingdom shine through us so brilliantly that we are open gateways of heaven for You to flow through and do mighty signs and wonders all for Your glory.

Jesus, Your Word says You keep us safe from every hidden trap of the enemy, so no matter what happens, we thank You for that. Give us unwavering tenacity and determined hearts to cling to You no matter what. We ask for mercy and grace to have joy in the trials and to feel Your presence even in our times of trouble.

Help us to never quit and to come through every storm clinging to You and shining brighter and brighter for Your glory. Your Word says You lead the righteous into the full light of day, from glory to glory. We thank You for Your truth and promises and for being so faithful and true. Please remove every block in us that prevents us from knowing You more and more.

We ask it in your name, Jesus.

Amen.

CLOSING PRAYER FOR YOU

I pray:

- Your spirit has been stirred and you have a heart on fire for God more than ever before

- You will experience a burning heart for God every day

- You will see God's hand in your life, hemming you in before and behind to His love and ways every day

- You will see God as your Father, Best Friend and Teacher

- The intimacy with God is restored in your life so you can walk with God as Adam did in the garden

- God's blessing and protection upon you and that your heart on fire would never dim, but only increase to the hottest, most glorious blue flame!

ABOUT THE AUTHOR

Zion Lucier is an author and avid pursuer of God. Her passion is to be as close to God as possible. She has received education through a school of ministry in Kelowna and it is out of these places and from the deep healing journey she has been on that God's whispers pierce her heart. A survivor of abuse, emotionally poignant lessons emerge from deep suffering. Join her on this daily journey walking in the freedom of truth.

Zion Lucier lives in Northern British Columbia with her husband surrounded by the inspiration of God's gorgeous wilderness, with time and space to spend in His presence.

www.zionlucier.com

ENDNOTES

DAY 6

1. Rick Joyner, The Torch and the Sword, Fort Mill: MorningStar Publications, E-book 2010, Loc 527-533

DAY 7

1. Brian Simmons (2013, Sept. 5) Passion and Fire Ministries. https://m.facebook.com/passiontranslation/posts/513452992066220

DAY 12

1. Footnote b – biblegateway.com for Psalm 23:3 TPT.

DAY 18

1. Footnote b – biblegateway.com for John 14:16, TPT.

DAY 26

1. Wendy Alec. Visions From Heaven: Visitations to my Father's Chamber. Dublin 2: Warboys Publishing (Ireland) Limited. Copyright 2013. Kindle for IOS. Loc 3046-3057.
2. Wendy Alec. Visions From Heaven: Visitations to my Father's Chamber. Dublin 2: Warboys Publishing (Ireland) Limited. Copyright 2013. Kindle for IOS. Loc 3057-3067.
3. Wendy Alec. Visions From Heaven: Visitations to my Father's Chamber. Dublin 2: Warboys Publishing (Ireland) Limited. Copyright 2013. Kindle for IOS. Loc 3076.

DAY 27

1. Footnote c – biblegateway.com for Romans 8:17b, TPT.

WORKS CITED

Joyner, Rick. Chapter 2 - The Messenger. *The Torch and the Sword* (E-Book Kindle for IOS). Loc 572-579. Copyright 2003; Ebook-2010. MorningStar Publication, Printed in United States of America

Wendy Alec. Chapter Name: The Great Sifting Before the Release of the Next Great Awakening. Book Name: *Visions From Heaven: Visitations to my Father's Chamber*. Dublin 2: Warboys Publishing (Ireland) Limited. Copyright 2013. Kindle for IOS. Loc 3046-3057.

Made in the USA
Middletown, DE
18 September 2020